BR

Burgers

KÖNEMANN

Chips

Chips, the favourite to accompany a mouthwatering hamburger. Crisp and hot, they will be devoured in no time.

Potato Ribbons

Peel 5–6 large potatoes. Wash thoroughly and pat dry with paper towels. Peel potatoes into ribbons using a vegetable peeler. Half fill a large pan with oil and heat oil to moderately hot. Cook ribbons in oil in batches for 3–4 minutes or until crisp and golden. Drain on paper towels. Serve ribbons hot, sprinkled with salt and pepper, or drizzled with sweet Thai chilli sauce.

The Perfect Chip

Peel 5–6 large potatoes. Wash thoroughly and pat dry with paper towels. Cut lengthways into 1 cm-wide slices and cut each slice into 1 cm-wide sticks. Half fill a large pan with oil and heat oil to moderately hot. Cook chips in oil, in batches, 4–5 minutes or until pale golden. Remove with tongs or a slotted spoon. Drain on paper towels. Reheat oil just prior to serving. Cook chips again for 2–3 minutes or until golden and crisp; drain. Sprinkle with salt for serving.

Crinkle Cut Chips

Prepare chips according to the Perfect Chip method described above, but use a crinkle potato cutter instead of a sharp knife. Half fill a large pan with oil and heat oil to moderately hot. Cook chips in oil, in batches, 4–5 minutes or until pale golden. Remove with tongs or a slotted spoon. Drain on paper towels. Reheat oil just prior to serving. Cook chips again for 2–3 minutes or until golden and crisp; drain. Sprinkle with salt, or use chicken salt or lemon pepper seasoning, if preferred.

Cheesy Potato Skins

Scrub 5–6 large potatoes and pat dry with paper towels. Do not peel. Prick each potato twice with a fork. Bake in moderately hot 210°C (gas 190°C) oven for 1 hour or until skins are crisp and flesh is soft. Turn once during cooking. Remove from oven; cool. Halve potatoes, scoop out flesh, leaving 5 mm of potato in shell. Cut each half into 3 wedges. Fill one-third of medium pan with oil, heat oil to moderately hot. Cook potato skins in batches 2–3 minutes or until crisp. Drain on paper towels. Serve sprinkled with very finely grated fresh parmesan cheese, cracked black pepper or a creamy dip.

French Fries

Peel 5–6 large potatoes. Wash and pat dry with paper towels. Cut lengthways into 5 mm-thin slices and cut each slice into 5 mm-wide sticks. Half fill a pan with oil, heat oil to moderately hot. Cook chips in batches 5–10 minutes or until crisp. Remove with slotted spoon. Drain on paper towels. Serve with tomato sauce or sprinkled with salt and vinegar.

Crispy Potato Wedges

Wash and scrub thoroughly 5–6 large potatoes. Cut each into about 10 wedges. Pat dry thoroughly with paper towels. Half fill a large pan with oil, heat oil to moderately hot. Add wedges and cook for 5–10 minutes or until golden-brown. Remove with tongs or slotted spoon. Drain on paper towels. Serve with combined 1/3 cup sour cream, 2 tablespoons mayonnaise, freshly chopped chives and parsley and salt and pepper to taste.

Potato Slices

Peel 5–6 medium potatoes. Wash and pat dry with paper towels. Cut potatoes into 5 mm slices using a sharp knife or a crinkle potato cutter. Half fill a large pan with oil and heat oil to moderately hot. Cook slices in oil, in batches, 5–10 minutes or until golden and lightly crisp. Drain on paper towels. Sprinkle with salt. Drizzle a little melted butter, combined with a crushed garlic clove, over top, if desired.

From left: Potato Ribbons, The Perfect Chip, Crinkle Cut Chips, Cheesy Potato Skins, French Fries, Crispy Potato Wedges, Potato Slices.

Burgers

Creative burgers can be made from a choice of meat, chicken, fish or vegetables and a variety of breads.

Aussie Burger

Preparation time:
  20 minutes
Total cooking time:
  15 minutes
Serves 4

500 g lean beef mince
1 onion, finely chopped
1 egg
$^1/_3$ cup breadcrumbs
2 tablespoons tomato
  sauce
1 teaspoon steak
  seasoning
salt and pepper to taste
40 g butter
2 large onions, extra,
  cut in thin rings
4 slices cheddar cheese
4 eggs, extra
4 rashers bacon, rind
  removed
4 large hamburger
  buns, halved
shredded lettuce
1 large tomato, sliced
4 large beetroot slices,
  drained
4 pineapple rings,
  drained
tomato sauce, for serving

1. Combine mince, chopped onion, egg, breadcrumbs, sauce, seasoning, salt and pepper in bowl. Mix with hands to combine. Divide mixture into 4 and shape into round patties. Heat 30 g butter in pan, add onion rings. Cook over medium heat until browned. Keep warm.
2. Heat a frying pan or grill plate, brush with oil. Cook patties 3–4 minutes each side or until cooked through. Place a cheese slice on each patty.
3. While patties are cooking, heat remaining butter in a frying pan. Fry eggs and bacon until eggs are cooked through and bacon is crisp.
4. Toast buns and place bases on serving plates. On each base, place lettuce, tomato, beetroot, pineapple, then a meat patty. Follow these with onion, bacon, egg and finally a bun top.

Aussie Burger.

Beef Sloppy Joe

Preparation time:
  10–15 minutes
Total cooking time:
  30–40 minutes
Serves 4

2 tablespoons olive oil
1 large onion, finely
  chopped
1 teaspoon beef stock
  powder
500 g lean beef mince
1 tablespoon
  worcestershire sauce
1/4 cup tomato sauce
1 tablespoon lemon
  juice
1/2 teaspoon salt
1 teaspoon dry English
  mustard powder
2 teaspoons soft brown
  sugar
1 tomato, roughly
  chopped
1/2 cup frozen peas
1/2 cup water
1 tablespoon cornflour
4 cheese buns
4 lettuce leaves
1/2 cup snow pea sprouts

1. Heat oil in frying
pan, add onion; cook
over medium heat
10 minutes or until
soft. Add stock and
mince, cook over high
heat until brown. Add
sauces, juice, salt,
mustard and sugar.
Stir-fry 3 minutes. Add
tomato and peas, cook
2 minutes.
2. Add half the water,
bring to boil. Reduce
heat to medium, cover
and cook 5 minutes.
Combine cornflour
with remaining water,
add to pan and stir
until mixture boils
and thickens.
3. Cut buns in half
horizontally, toast cut
side and butter lightly.
Place bun bases on
4 serving plates. On
each base place lettuce,
sprouts, beef mixture
and finally a bun top.
May be served with
cheesy potato skins.

Southern Fried Chicken Fillet Burger with Garlic Mayonnaise

Preparation time:
  40 minutes
Total cooking time:
  5–8 minutes
Serves 4

1/3 cup whole egg
  mayonnaise
1 clove garlic, crushed
1 egg yolk
1 teaspoon lemon juice
1/2 teaspoon grated
  lemon rind
4 chicken fillets
1/2 cup plain flour
1 tablespoon chicken
  stock powder
3/4 teaspoon celery salt
1/2 teaspoon garlic
  powder
1/2 teaspoon ground
  white pepper
2 tablespoons cornflake
  crumbs
1 tablespoon polenta
oil for shallow frying
4 large sesame seed
  rolls
lettuce leaves
1 tomato, thinly sliced

1. To make garlic
mayonnaise, combine
mayonnaise, garlic, yolk,
juice and rind in small
bowl. Whisk until well
combined.
2. Trim chicken of excess
fat and sinew. Combine
flour, stock, celery salt,
garlic, pepper, cornflake
crumbs and polenta on
sheet of greaseproof
paper. Dip chicken fillets
in water and coat well
with flour mixture.
3. Heat oil in large
heavy-based frying pan.
Cook coated chicken
3–4 minutes each side or
until golden and cooked
through. Remove and
drain on paper towels.
4. Cut rolls in half
horizontally. Lightly
toast and butter if
desired. Place roll bases
on 4 serving plates. On
each base place lettuce
leaves, tomato, chicken
fillet, a spoonful of garlic
mayonnaise and finally
a roll top.

*Beef Sloppy Joe (top) and Southern Fried Chicken
Fillet Burger with Garlic Mayonnaise.*

Lamb Burger with Minted Yoghurt Sauce

Preparation time:
25 minutes +
15 minutes standing
Total cooking time:
5–10 minutes
Serves 4

Minted Yoghurt Sauce
3/4 cup plain yoghurt
1 tablespoon chopped
fresh mint
1/4 teaspoon ground
cumin
1 teaspoon soft brown
sugar

500 g lamb fillets
salt and pepper
1 teaspoon ground
cumin
1/4 teaspoon sweet
paprika
1 tablespoon olive oil
30 g butter
1–2 cloves garlic, crushed
1 teaspoon grated
lemon rind
8 small round pitta
breads, toasted
4 egg tomatoes, thinly
sliced
salt and cracked black
pepper, extra
green mango chutney,
optional

**1. *To make minted
yoghurt sauce:*** Place
yoghurt, mint, cumin
and sugar in small bowl.
Stir to combine.

2. Trim lamb of excess
fat and sinew. Combine
salt, pepper, cumin and
paprika. Rub evenly
over lamb. Cover and
stand 15 minutes.

3. Heat oil and butter
in frying pan. Add
garlic and lemon rind,
cook 1 minute. Add
lamb fillets. Cook over
medium heat 4–5
minutes or until brown
and tender. For well
done lamb, continue
cooking 2–3 minutes.
Remove from pan,
cover with foil, stand
5 minutes.

4. Place 4 pitta breads
on serving plates and
place tomato slices on
each. Thinly slice lamb
and lay over tomato.
Sprinkle with salt and
freshly cracked black
pepper. Spoon sauce
over, followed by
remaining pitta bread.
Serve with green mango
chutney if desired.

> HINT
> Pitta is a round flat
> two-layered bread.
> If you like it warm,
> heat it briefly in a
> slow oven or under
> a warm grill.

Indian Chicken Burger

Preparation time:
20 minutes +
refrigeration
Total cooking time:
10 minutes
Serves 4

1/2 cup plain yoghurt
2 teaspoons grated
fresh ginger
1 tablespoon soft
brown sugar
1 teaspoon ground
turmeric
1 teaspoon ground
cumin
2 teaspoons tandoori
powder
1 clove garlic, crushed
1 tablespoon tomato
sauce
4 chicken breast fillets
oil for frying
1 medium Lebanese
cucumber
1 banana, thinly sliced
diagonally
1 tablespoon lemon
juice
4 naan bread
lettuce leaves
1/4 cup mango chutney
1/4 cup flaked or
shredded coconut,
toasted

1. Combine yoghurt,
ginger, sugar, turmeric,
cumin, tandoori
powder, garlic and
tomato sauce in
medium bowl. Mix
well. Trim chicken of

Lamb Burger with Minted Yoghurt Sauce (top) and Indian Chicken Burger.

excess fat and sinew. Add to yoghurt mixture, stirring to coat. Refrigerate, covered for up to 3 hours.
2. Heat a little oil in large frying pan. Add chicken, cook over medium heat 3–4 minutes each side or until brown and cooked through.
3. While chicken is cooking, use a vegetable peeler to peel cucumber into thin ribbon strips. Coat banana slices in lemon juice. Place naan bread on individual serving plates. On one half of each, place lettuce, cucumber ribbons, banana slices and chicken. Top with chutney and sprinkle with coconut. Fold naan bread over to enclose filling. Serve.

Club Burger

Preparation time:
20 minutes
Total cooking time:
5–10 minutes
Serves 4

6 thick rashers bacon,
  cut in 3 cm pieces
30 g butter
100 g button
  mushrooms, sliced
cracked pepper
4 wholemeal bread
  rolls
green oak leaf or butter
  lettuce
1 large ripe tomato,
  thinly sliced
1 firm ripe avocado,
  peeled and thinly
  sliced
1/4 cup fresh basil
  leaves
whole egg mayonnaise,
  optional

1. Place bacon pieces
in an ungreased frying
pan, cook over medium
heat until crisp. Drain
on paper towels; keep
warm. Add butter,
sliced mushrooms and
pepper to pan. Cook,
stirring 2–3 minutes or
until brown. Remove
pan from heat.
2. Cut rolls in half
horizontally. Lightly
toast cut sides if desired.
Place roll bases on
4 serving plates. On
each base place lettuce
leaves, tomato,
avocado, bacon,
mushrooms, basil leaves
and a dollop of
mayonnaise if using.
Finish with a roll top.

Veal Burger with Avocado and Cheese

Preparation time:
25 minutes
Total cooking time:
10–12 minutes
Serves 4

500 g lean veal mince
1 teaspoon salt
1/2 teaspoon white
  pepper
1 clove garlic, crushed
2 tablespoons cream
1 tablespoon tomato
  paste
1 tablespoon light olive
  oil
1 tablespoon oil
1 firm ripe avocado,
  peeled and thinly sliced
1/2 cup grated cheddar
  cheese
2 tablespoons freshly
  grated parmesan cheese
4 large squares of olive
  focaccia
1 small bunch rocket,
  torn into pieces
snow pea sprouts
lime juice

1. Combine mince, salt,
pepper, garlic and
cream in medium bowl.
Mix with hands until
well combined. Divide
mixture into 4 portions
and shape into round
patties.
2. Combine tomato
paste and light olive oil
in small bowl; set aside.
Heat remaining oil in
large frying pan. Cook
patties 3–4 minutes
each side or until brown
and cooked through.
Remove patties from
frying pan, drain on
paper towels.
3. Place patties on a
foil-lined grill tray. Top
each with overlapping
slices of avocado. Brush
each with tomato paste
mixture. Sprinkle with
combined cheeses.
Cook under preheated
grill for 1–2 minutes or
until cheese has melted.
4. Cut each focaccia in
half horizontally.
Lightly toast cut sides if
desired. Place bases of
focaccia on 4 serving
plates. On each base,
place rocket pieces and
snow pea sprouts.
Sprinkle with a little
lime juice. Place a meat
and avocado patty on
top of each base,
followed by remaining
half of focaccia.

Club Burger (top) and Veal Burger with Avocado
and Cheese.

1. *Add soy sauce to other ingredients in bowl and mix well with a spoon.*

2. *Stir in red capsicum, carrot, bok choy, extra ginger and chilli sauce.*

Vegetable Omelette Burger

Preparation time:
40 minutes
Total cooking time:
10–15 minutes
Serves 4

4 baby beetroot, peeled
  and grated
1/2 teaspoon grated
  fresh ginger
1 small clove garlic,
  crushed
1 teaspoon rice
  vinegar
1 teaspoon sesame oil
1 teaspoon soy sauce
2 spring onions, finely
  chopped
Tabasco sauce
  to taste
1/4 cup peanut oil
1 onion, thinly sliced
1 clove garlic, crushed,
  extra,
1 red capsicum, cut in
  thin strips

1 medium carrot,
  peeled and grated
4 baby bok choy leaves,
  shredded
2 teaspoons fresh
  grated ginger, extra
1 tablespoon sweet
  chilli sauce
3 eggs, lightly beaten
1 tablespoon cornflour
3–4 teaspoons soy
  sauce, extra
8 round pitta breads
yellow capsicum, thinly
  sliced, for serving,
  optional

1. Place beetroot, ginger, garlic, rice vinegar, sesame oil, soy sauce, spring onion and Tabasco in a medium bowl. Mix until well combined and set aside.
2. Heat half the peanut oil in a wok or frying pan. Add onion and extra garlic, cook over medium heat 1 minute. Stir in red capsicum strips, carrot, bok choy, extra ginger and chilli sauce. Cook for another 1–2 minutes or until just tender. Remove from heat and transfer mixture to a large bowl. Allow to cool slightly. Combine eggs, cornflour and extra soy sauce in a bowl. Add to cooled mixture; stir well.
3. Heat remaining oil in frying pan. Spoon one-quarter of the mixture into pan to make a thick round. Cook 1–2 minutes each side. Repeat with remaining mixture using one-quarter at a time.
4. Lightly toast pitta breads on both sides. Drain excess liquid from beetroot mixture. Place 4 pitta breads on individual serving plates. On each bread, place a vegetable omelette and some beetroot mixture. Garnish with yellow capsicum, if desired. Serve with remaining pitta bread.

Vegetable Omelette Burger.

3. Spoon one-quarter of mixture into pan and cook for 1–2 minutes each side.

4. Lightly toast pitta breads on both sides, using a grill or toaster.

13

Lamb and Feta Cheese Burger

Preparation time:
20 minutes
Total cooking time:
10–15 minutes
Serves 4

1 bunch spring onions
1 tablespoon olive oil
2 tablespoons soft
  brown sugar
400 g lamb fillets
2 cloves garlic, crushed
1 teaspoon chopped
  fresh rosemary
4 long crusty rolls,
  halved
80 g feta cheese, sliced
  thinly
1/3 cup fresh mint
  leaves

1. Cut onions in half and cook in a pan of boiling water for 2–3 minutes or until tender. Drain. Heat oil in frying pan, add onions and sugar, cook over medium heat until soft and golden.
2. Rub lamb fillets with garlic, sprinkle with rosemary, place under preheated grill. Cook fillets under high heat 4–5 minutes, turning frequently, until well-browned on outside, pink inside. Stand for 2–3 minutes, thinly slice diagonally.
3. Toast rolls on cut sides, butter if desired.

Place roll bases on 4 serving plates. On each base place lamb slices, feta, onion, mint leaves and finally a roll top. May be served with a mixed salad and garnished with herbs of your choice.

Beef and Mushroom Burger

Preparation time:
20 minutes
Total cooking time:
10 minutes
Serves 4

500 g lean beef mince
1/2 teaspoon salt
1 teaspoon ground
  black pepper
2–3 tablespoons finely
  chopped fresh parsley
2 tablespoons red wine
1 teaspoon soft brown
  sugar
1 small onion, grated
2–3 tablespoons oil
45 g butter
1–2 cloves garlic,
  crushed
250 g small button
  mushrooms,
  thinly sliced
1/4 cup sour cream or
  2–3 tablespoons
  cream
2–3 teaspoons marsala
4 poppy seed rolls
chopped fresh basil or
  parsley, extra

1. Combine mince, salt, pepper, parsley, wine, sugar and onion in medium bowl. Mix with hands until well combined. Divide mixture into 4 portions and shape into patties.
2. Heat oil in large frying pan. Add patties, cook over medium heat 3–4 minutes each side or until brown and cooked through. Remove from pan; keep warm. Add butter, garlic and mushrooms to pan. Cook over medium heat until mushrooms are tender and brown. Stir in cream and marsala, cook 2–3 more minutes or until liquid has reduced slightly.
3. Cut rolls in half horizontally and lightly toast cut sides. Butter cut sides if desired. On each base, place a meat patty and spoon mushroom mixture over the top. Sprinkle with extra chopped parsley or basil and finish with the top half of the roll. May be served with French fries and garnished with herbs.

Lamb and Feta Cheese Burger (top)
and Beef and Mushroom Burger.

Mexican Burger with Guacamole

Preparation time:
  30 minutes
Total cooking time:
  10–15 minutes
Serves 4

Guacamole
1 medium ripe avocado
1 small ripe tomato,
  peeled and finely
  chopped
1 clove garlic, crushed
1/2 small onion, finely
  chopped
1 tablespoon lemon
  juice
1 tablespoon finely
  chopped fresh
  coriander

1 tablespoon oil
3 teaspoons chilli oil
1 large onion, finely
  chopped
500 g lean beef mince
1/2 teaspoon chilli
  powder
1 teaspoon ground
  cumin
1/2 teaspoon salt
1 cup grated cheddar
  cheese
1/4 cup oil, extra
4 flour tortillas, halved
1 cup shredded lettuce
1 tomato, thinly sliced
1/2 cup bottled tomato
  salsa

1. To make guacamole:
Cut avocado in half,
remove seed. Peel
avocado and place flesh

in a bowl. Mash well
with a fork. Add
tomato, garlic, onion,
juice and coriander to
bowl. Mix to combine.
Set aside.
2. Heat combined oils
in large pan. Add
onion, cook over
medium heat 3–4
minutes or until
golden. Remove from
heat; cool slightly.
Combine onion, mince,
chilli, cumin, salt,
1/2 cup cheese in
medium bowl. Mix
with hands until well
combined. Divide
mixture into 4 portions
and shape into round
patties; flatten slightly.
3. Reheat frying pan,
adding a little extra oil
if necessary. Cook meat
patties over medium
heat 3–4 minutes each
side or until brown and
cooked through.
4. While patties are
cooking, heat extra oil
in another pan. Place
1 tablespoon cheese on
one half of each piece
of tortilla. Fold tortillas
over, press down and
fry until golden on each
side. Place tortilla
halves on serving
plates. On 4 of them,
place lettuce, tomato,
a meat patty, tomato
salsa and prepared
guacamole.

Note: The cheese holds
the tortillas together
while frying.

Steak Diane Burger

Preparation time:
  25 minutes
Total cooking time:
  10 minutes
Serves 4

4 x 150 g fillet or rump
  steaks
1 tablespoon oil
50 g butter
1–2 cloves garlic, crushed
1 large onion, cut in
  thin rings
1 tablespoon
  worcestershire sauce
1 tablespoon tomato
  sauce
2 tablespoons sour
  cream
2 tablespoons finely
  chopped fresh parsley
4 seed rolls
1 teaspoon peanut oil
Tabasco to taste
160 g mesclun (mixed
  salad greens)
100 g snow peas,
  trimmed, blanched
  and sliced

1. Trim meat of excess
fat and sinew. Flatten
steaks to an even
thickness using a meat
mallet or rolling pin.
Heat oil in frying pan.
Add steaks, cook over
medium heat 2 minutes
each side or until
brown on the outside
and pink in the centre.
Remove steaks from
pan; set aside, cover
and keep warm.

Steak Diane Burger (top) and Mexican Burger with Guacamole.

2. Add butter and garlic to pan, cook 1 minute. Stir in onion; cook over medium heat 3–4 minutes or until soft. Remove from pan, keep warm. Stir in sauces, sour cream and parsley. Return meat to pan, turn to coat meat

all over with sauce. **3.** Cut rolls in half horizontally and toast cut sides. Spread with butter if desired. Place roll bases on serving plates. On each base place combined peanut oil, Tabasco and mesclun or salad mix.

Add snow peas, steak, fried onion and finally a roll top.

Note: To blanch snow peas, plunge in hot water and then in iced water. This will enhance the colour and slightly soften the texture.

17

Corned Beef Hashburger

Preparation time:
  20 minutes
Total cooking time:
  10 minutes
Serves 4

1 large potato (150 g),
  peeled and grated
250 g cooked corned
  beef, cut in thin strips
1 egg, lightly beaten
1/2 teaspoon ground
  black pepper
2 tablespoons cream
1 teaspoon horseradish
30 g butter
1 tablespoon oil
4 eggs, extra
1/2 cup grated cheddar
  cheese
1 large French stick
green coral lettuce
1/4 cup mild pickled
  peppers, finely
  sliced
barbecue sauce

1. Place potato in
muslin or fine strainer
and squeeze out excess
moisture. Combine
potato, corned beef,
egg, pepper, cream and
horseradish in medium
bowl. Mix well. Divide
combined mixture into
4 portions and shape
into long patties.
2. Heat butter and half
the oil in large frying
pan. Add patties, cook
over medium heat
3–4 minutes each side

or until golden brown
and lightly crisp. Drain
on paper towels.
3. While patties are
cooking, heat
remaining oil in
medium frying pan.
Break eggs into pan.
Cook over medium
heat until almost set.
Sprinkle cheese over
each and cook until
cheese melts.
4. Cut bread stick into
4 sections. Split each
in half horizontally
and lightly toast cut
side. Spread with
butter if desired. Place
bread bases on serving
plates. On each base
place a lettuce leaf, a
patty, an egg, pickled
peppers, sauce and
remaining bread.

Pepper Burger with Caramelised Onions

Preparation time:
  20 minutes
Total cooking time:
  20 minutes
Serves 4

550 g lean beef
  mince
1/2 teaspoon salt

2 tablespoons chopped
  fresh parsley
2 tablespoons drained
  green peppercorns
1 tablespoon cracked
  black pepper
30 g butter
3 large white onions,
  peeled and thinly
  sliced in rings
1 tablespoon soft
  brown sugar
4 large damper rolls
green butter lettuce
1/3 cup sour cream
1 tablespoon
  wholegrain mustard
1 clove garlic,
  crushed

1. Combine mince,
salt, 1 tablespoon
parsley, peppercorns
and cracked pepper in
large bowl. Mix with
hands until well
combined. Divide
mince mixture into
4 portions and shape
into round patties.
Cover and set aside.
2. Heat butter in large
frying pan. Add onion
and cook over
medium-low heat
until a deep caramel
colour, stirring
occasionally to prevent
burning. Add brown
sugar and cook,
stirring until onions
are well browned but
not burnt. Remove
from heat. Transfer to
a plate, cover and
keep warm.
3. Using the same pan,
cook meat patties over

Pepper Burger with Caramelised Onions (top) and Corned Beef Hashburger.

medium heat for 5–6 minutes each side or until well browned and cooked through. Cut damper rolls in half horizontally.

Toast, and place roll bases on 4 serving plates. On each base, place a lettuce leaf, a patty and some onion. Spoon a dollop of

combined sour cream, wholegrain mustard and garlic over onions. Sprinkle with remaining parsley and finish with a roll top.

19

Prawn Burger with Cocktail Sauce

Preparation time:
35 minutes +
refrigeration
Total cooking time:
5–10 minutes
Serves 4

8 large green prawns
2 tablespoons lemon or
  lime juice
1 tablespoon sesame seeds
1¹/2 cups fresh white
  breadcrumbs
2 tablespoons finely
  chopped fresh coriander
1 egg, lightly beaten
2 teaspoons chilli sauce
plain flour for dusting
¹/4 cup olive oil
¹/3 cup whole egg
  mayonnaise
1 spring onion, finely
  chopped
1 tablespoon tomato
  sauce
1 teaspoon
  worcestershire sauce
chilli sauce, extra

1 tablespoon lemon or
  lime juice, extra
4 hamburger buns,
  halved
rocket lettuce
¹/2 small bunch
  watercress
1 firm ripe avocado,
  peeled and thinly sliced
1 teaspoon cracked
  pepper

1. Peel prawns and discard shells. Cut prawns lengthways down the back almost all the way through. Remove vein. Flatten prawns slightly. Combine prawns and lemon or lime juice; mix well.

2. Combine sesame seeds, breadcrumbs and coriander on a sheet of greaseproof paper. Combine egg and chilli sauce in a bowl. Dust prawns lightly in flour; shake off excess. Dip prawns in egg mixture and then press firmly in breadcrumb mixture to coat. Place prawns on tray, cover, refrigerate 10 minutes.

3. Heat oil in frying pan. Add prawns and cook over medium heat 2–3 minutes each side. Remove from pan, drain on paper towels. Combine mayonnaise, spring onion, tomato and worcestershire sauces, extra chilli sauce and extra lemon or lime juice in bowl.

4. Toast and butter each bun lightly. Place bun bases on 4 serving plates. On each base place rocket, watercress and avocado. Sprinkle with the cracked pepper. Add 2 prawns, some cocktail sauce and finally a bun top. May be served with crinkle cut chips and garnished with sprigs of dill, if desired.

Prawn Burger with Cocktail Sauce.

1. Cut prawns lengthways down the back almost all the way through. Remove vein.

2. Dust prawns in flour, dip in egg mixture and press firmly in crumb mix.

3. *Combine mayonnaise, onion, sauces and extra juice in a bowl.*

4. *Place rocket, watercress and avocado on buns. Add 2 cooked prawns.*

Mustard Burger with Garlic Butter

Preparation time:
25 minutes +
refrigeration
Total cooking time:
10 minutes
Serves 4

Garlic Butter
60 g butter, softened
1–2 cloves garlic,
  crushed
1/4 cup chopped fresh
  parsley

500 g lean beef mince
1/2 teaspoon salt
1/2 teaspoon pepper
1–2 tablespoons Dijon
  mustard

2 large red capsicum
oil
4 rolls, halved
2 small Lebanese
  cucumbers, thinly
  sliced lengthways

**1. To make garlic
butter:** Using electric
beaters, beat butter
until light and creamy.
Add garlic and parsley.

Place on a piece of foil or plastic wrap. Roll up and refrigerate until firm.

2. Combine mince, salt, pepper and mustard in large bowl. Mix with hands until well combined. Divide the mixture into 4 portions and shape each into a round patty. Cover patties, set aside.

3. Cut both capsicum in half; remove seeds and membrane. Place skin side up on cold grill tray. Brush with oil. Cook under preheated grill until skin is black. Remove; cover with damp tea-towel until cool. Peel away skin. Cut flesh in 2 cm strips.

4. Heat a large frying pan or grill plate, brush liberally with oil. Cook meat patties 3–4 minutes each side or until brown and cooked through. Lightly toast cut sides of rolls and place bases on 4 serving plates. On each base place cucumber slices and capsicum strips, followed by a meat patty. Slice butter log into rounds and place 1 or 2 on each patty. Finish with roll tops. May be garnished with sprigs of fresh parsley or other herbs.

Mediterranean Vegetable and Goats Cheese Burger

Preparation time:
  30 minutes +
  20 minutes standing
Total cooking time:
  15–20 minutes
Serves 4

400 g eggplant, thinly
  sliced
salt
1 red capsicum, halved,
  seeds and membrane
  removed
1/2 cup olive oil
3 cloves garlic, chopped
1 red chilli, finely
  chopped
4 fresh basil leaves,
  shredded
100 g zucchini, thinly
  sliced lengthways
100 g sweet potato,
  peeled and thinly
  sliced
4 seed rolls
100 g goats cheese
mesclun (mixed salad
  greens)
balsamic vinegar

1. Spread eggplant slices on a board, sprinkle well with salt and leave to stand for 20 minutes. Place in a colander or strainer and rinse.

Pat dry with paper towels and set aside.

2. Place capsicum on grill tray skin side up. Cook under preheated grill until skin is black. Remove and cover with a damp tea-towel and allow to cool. Peel away skin and cut flesh into thick strips.

3. Heat 1/4 cup of oil in frying pan and cook eggplant slices until golden on both sides. Heat remaining oil in pan, add garlic, chilli and basil. Add zucchini and sweet potato and cook until soft and golden. Remove and strain. Reserve any oil.

4. Cut rolls in half, toast each side. Spread bases with goats cheese and cook under preheated grill for 1 minute or until cheese has melted. Place on 4 serving plates. Arrange salad greens on top of cheese. Layer eggplant, capsicum, sweet potato and zucchini over salad. Sprinkle lightly with balsamic vinegar and reserved oil, top with remaining rolls.

*Mustard Burger with Garlic Butter (top) and
Mediterranean Vegetable and Goats Cheese Burger.*

Salmon and Avocado Burger

Preparation time:
  30 minutes +
  2 hours refrigeration
Total cooking time:
  10–15 minutes
Serves 4

2 medium potatoes,
  peeled and chopped
125 g pumpkin, peeled
  and chopped
310 g can pink or red
  salmon, drained
1 small onion, grated,
  drained of excess
  moisture
1/2 teaspoon salt
1/2 teaspoon white
  pepper
1 egg
1 egg yolk, extra
11/2 cups breadcrumbs
2 tablespoons chopped
  fresh dill
1/4 cup oil
1 firm ripe avocado,
  roughly chopped
1/4 cup finely chopped
  red capsicum
2 tablespoons lemon
  juice
1 tablespoon whole egg
  mayonnaise
4 oval pocket bread
radicchio lettuce

1. Cook potato in
medium pan of boiling
water until soft; drain
well. Steam or
microwave pumpkin
until tender, drain.
Combine potato and
pumpkin in medium
bowl; mash with a fork
until well combined.
Add salmon, onion,
salt, pepper, lightly
beaten egg and extra
egg yolk, and 1 cup of
breadcrumbs. Stir until
well combined. Divide
mixture into 4 portions
and shape into round
patties. Combine
remaining breadcrumbs
with dill and use to
coat each patty. Cover
and refrigerate
for up to 2 hours.
2. Heat oil in large
frying pan. Add patties,
cook over medium heat
for 3–4 minutes each
side or until golden
brown and cooked
through.
3. Combine avocado,
capsicum, lemon juice
and mayonnaise. Split
pocket breads in half,
fill each with lettuce
leaves, a patty and
avocado mixture.

Steak and Onion Burger

Preparation time:
  25 minutes
Total cooking time:
  15–20 minutes
Serves 4

2 tablespoons olive oil
3 large onions, thinly
  sliced
3 teaspoons sugar
1 cup red wine
2 teaspoons
  worcestershire sauce
1 clove garlic, crushed
4 fillet or scotch fillet
  steaks
salt and pepper to taste
1 cup grated carrot
1/4 teaspoon cracked
  black pepper, extra
1/4 cup flaked almonds
1 tablespoon
  mayonnaise
2 baby beetroot, peeled
  and grated
1 tablespoon white
  wine vinegar
1/2 teaspoon sugar,
  extra
4 fancy bread rolls
mignonette lettuce

1. Heat oil in medium
pan. Add onion, cook
over medium heat 4–5
minutes or until onion
is soft. Add sugar;
increase heat. Cook,
stirring until onion is
golden brown. Pour in
wine. Bring to boil,
continue boiling until
all wine is absorbed.
Add worcestershire
sauce and garlic and
stir through; cook
30 seconds. Remove
from heat, keep warm.
2. Trim meat of excess
fat and sinew. Cook
steaks under a preheated
grill 3–4 minutes each
side or in a frying pan
over a medium heat,
until steaks are cooked
to taste. Sprinkle with
salt and pepper if desired.
3. Combine carrot,
extra pepper, almonds

Steak and Onion Burger (top) and Salmon and Avocado Burger.

and mayonnaise in a small bowl; mix well. Combine beetroot, vinegar and extra sugar in another bowl; mix.

4. Cut rolls in half. Place 4 roll halves on individual serving plates. On each place lettuce leaves and a

steak, followed by onion, carrot and beetroot mixtures. Serve with remaining bread roll halves.

25

Cheese and Ham Burger with Polenta

Preparation time:
  20 minutes +
  refrigeration
Total cooking time:
  10–15 minutes
Serves 4

Polenta
1 cup water
1/2 cup polenta
  (cornmeal)
30 g butter
1/2 cup finely grated
  parmesan cheese
1 teaspoon chilli
  powder
1/4 cup soft cream cheese
1/2 red capsicum, finely
  chopped

500 g lean beef mince
1/4 cup breadcrumbs
2 tablespoons milk
1 teaspoon salt
1/2 teaspoon ground
  black pepper
100 g ham, finely
  chopped
1/2 cup grated cheddar
  or Jarlsberg cheese
2 tablespoons currants
2 teaspoons Mexican
  chilli powder
1 tablespoon oil
4 muffins
300 g English spinach
  leaves, finely shredded
2 tablespoons sour cream
2 tablespoons finely
  sliced mild pickled
  peppers

1. *To make polenta:*
Brush a bar tin with oil,
line with foil. Place
water in large pan.
Bring to boil, add
polenta, cook over
medium heat 5 minutes
or until mixture boils
and thickens. Stir in
butter, parmesan, chilli
powder, cream cheese
and capsicum. Mix
until well combined.
Spread mixture in
prepared bar tin, cool.
Turn mixture out,
remove foil. Cut into
thin slices.
2. Combine mince,
breadcrumbs, milk, salt,
pepper, ham, cheese,
currants and chilli
powder in medium
bowl. Mix with hands
until well combined.
Divide mixture into
4 portions and shape
into round patties,
flatten slightly. Cover
and refrigerate
for up to 3 hours
or overnight.
3. Heat oil in large
frying pan, add patties.
Cook over medium heat
3–4 minutes each side
or until brown and
cooked through.
4. Cut muffins in half
horizontally and toast
lightly. Place bottom
halves on serving
plates. On each, place
shredded spinach, a
patty, sour cream,
polenta slices, and
pickled peppers. Top
with other half of muffin.

Chicken and Asparagus Burger

Preparation time:
  25 minutes
Total cooking time:
  10 minutes
Serves 4

4 chicken breast fillets
1/2 teaspoon salt
1/4 teaspoon ground
  black pepper
1 tablespoon finely
  grated parmesan cheese
1/3 cup plain flour
1/4 teaspoon Tabasco
  sauce
2 tablespoons
  mayonnaise
1 tablespoon lime juice
1/2 teaspoon grated lime
  rind
2 tablespoons light
  olive oil
30 g butter
Tabasco sauce, extra
310 g can asparagus
  spears, drained
125 g camembert
  cheese, thinly sliced
sweet paprika
4 damper rolls
watercress
chives for garnish,
  optional

1. Trim chicken of
excess fat and sinew.
Flatten slightly with a
meat mallet or rolling
pin. Combine salt,
pepper, parmesan and
flour on a sheet of
greaseproof paper. Dust
chicken in flour mixture;

26

Cheese and Ham Burger with Polenta (top) and Chicken and Asparagus Burger.

shake off any excess.
2. Combine Tabasco, mayonnaise, lime juice and rind in small bowl. Set aside. Heat oil and butter in large frying pan. When butter begins to foam, add extra drops of Tabasco. Add chicken, cook over medium heat 2–3 minutes each side or

until golden and cooked through.
3. Transfer chicken to foil-lined grill tray. Spread mayonnaise mixture over each fillet. Arrange asparagus spears over the top. Place slices of camembert over asparagus, sprinkle with paprika. Cook under preheated grill

1–2 minutes or until cheese has melted.
4. Cut rolls in half horizontally. Lightly toast cut sides if desired. Place roll bases on 4 serving plates. On each base place some watercress, chicken and toppings, chives if used, and finally a roll top.

27

Turkey Burger with Spiced Cranberry Sauce

Preparation time:
  30–40 minutes
Total cooking time:
  20 minutes
Serves 4

Spiced Cranberry Sauce
20 g butter
*1/2 small onion, finely
  chopped*
2 teaspoons honey
*1/4 teaspoon mixed
  spice*
*1/2 teaspoon ground
  ginger*
1/3 cup cranberry sauce
1 teaspoon balsamic
  vinegar

*500 g turkey breast
  fillets*
*2 tablespoons finely
  chopped chives*
1 egg, lightly beaten
*1 clove garlic,
  crushed*
salt and pepper
2/3 cup breadcrumbs
oil for frying
*1 sourdough bread loaf
  or rye bread*
*mignonette lettuce for
  serving*
*8 thin slices mozzarella
  cheese*

**1. *To make spiced
cranberry sauce:*** Heat
butter in small pan, add
onion. Cook over
medium heat 3–4

minutes or until soft.
Stir in honey, spice and
ginger; cook 1 more
minute. Add cranberry
sauce and vinegar.
Simmer gently 2–3
minutes. Remove from
heat and cool slightly.
2. Trim turkey of excess
fat and sinew; chop
roughly. Place turkey in
food processor and
process 20–30 seconds
or until finely chopped.
Combine in large bowl
with chives, egg, garlic,
salt, pepper and
breadcrumbs. Mix with
wetted hands until well
combined. Divide
mixture into 4 and
shape into patties.
3. Heat a small amount
of oil in large heavy-
based frying pan. Cook
patties over medium
heat 3–4 minutes each
side or until golden and
cooked through. Drain
on paper towels.
Keep warm.
4. Cut bread loaf into
8 slices and lightly toast
and butter if desired.
Place 4 slices on serving
plates. On each slice
place lettuce leaves, a
patty, cheese, spiced
cranberry sauce and
finally a piece of toast.

Veal Schnitzel Burger

Preparation time:
  20 minutes
Total cooking time:
  5–10 minutes
Serves 4

*4 veal steaks,
  approximately 130 g
  each*
1/2 cup breadcrumbs
1 teaspoon lemon rind
*1 tablespoon grated
  parmesan cheese*
*1/2–1 teaspoon fresh
  finely chopped
  rosemary or chives*
plain flour
salt and pepper
1 egg, lightly beaten
30 g butter
1 tablespoon olive oil
1 clove garlic, crushed
8 slices thick crusty bread
*softened cream cheese
  for spreading*
*1 cup finely shredded
  English spinach leaves*
*1/4 cup finely shredded
  fresh basil leaves*
lemon juice for serving
lemon wedges, optional

1. Trim veal of excess
fat and sinew. On a
plate, combine
breadcrumbs, rind,
cheese and rosemary or
chives. Toss veal in
seasoned flour, dip in
egg, coat with
breadcrumb mixture.
2. Heat butter, oil and
crushed garlic in large

Turkey Burger with Spiced Cranberry Sauce (left) and Veal Schnitzel Burger.

heavy-based frying pan. Cook veal over medium heat 2–3 minutes each side or until golden and cooked through. Drain on paper towels.

3. Lightly toast bread slices on each side. Place 4 slices on individual serving plates and spread a little cream cheese on each slice. Place combined spinach and basil on top.

Squeeze a little lemon juice over veal, place veal on top of spinach and basil. Finish with remaining toast. Garnish with lemon wedges, if desired.

29

Hawaiian Teriyaki Burger

Preparation time:
20 minutes
Total cooking time:
15 minutes
Serves 4

2 cloves garlic, crushed
1 tablespoon soft
 brown sugar
1/2 teaspoon ground
 black pepper
3 teaspoons grated
 fresh ginger
2 tablespoons fresh
 chopped coriander
1/2 cup teriyaki marinade
1 small onion, finely
 grated
500 g lean beef mince
1 tablespoon peanut oil
4 small thin slices fresh
 pineapple or canned
 pineapple rings
1 tablespoon sesame oil
1 red onion, thinly
 sliced
2 slender baby
 eggplant, thinly sliced
 lengthways
1 small red capsicum,
 cut in thin strips
1 banana chilli, thinly
 sliced in rounds
1 tablespoon balsamic
 vinegar
1 large damper

1. Combine crushed
garlic, sugar, pepper,
ginger and half the
chopped coriander
with teriyaki marinade
in a small bowl.

Reserve 1/2 cup of the
mixture and set aside.
Add onion and mince
to the remaining
mixture. Mix with
hands until well
combined. Divide
mixture into 4 portions
and shape into round
patties.
2. Heat peanut oil in a
large frying pan. Cook
patties 3–4 minutes
each side or until they
are brown and cooked
through. Remove from
pan, keep warm. Cook
pineapple slices in the
same pan or on a
preheated grill plate.
Brush with reserved
marinade mixture
while cooking.
3. Heat sesame oil in
large frying pan. Add
onion, eggplant,
capsicum and chilli.
Cook over medium
heat 2–3 minutes or
until just softened. Stir
in remaining coriander
and balsamic vinegar.
Remove from heat.
4. Cut damper into
quarters and halve the
quarters horizontally.
Lightly toast and
butter damper, if
desired. Place the base
of each quarter slice of
damper on a serving
plate. On each base
place a meat patty,
slice of pineapple and
fried vegetables.
Finally, top with the
remaining quarters of
sliced damper.

Chicken Sloppy Joe

Preparation time:
25 minutes
Total cooking time:
25 minutes
Serves 4

500 g chicken breast
 fillets, chopped
1/4 cup light olive or
 mustard seed oil
1 clove garlic, crushed
1 large onion, finely
 chopped
1 small leek, finely sliced
250 g flat mushrooms,
 thinly sliced
2 teaspoons sweet
 paprika
salt and pepper to taste
1 tablespoon plain
 flour
3/4 cup milk
210 g can creamed
 corn
1 tablespoon chopped
 fresh mint
2 tablespoons sweet
 chilli sauce
4 fresh or frozen pizza
 bases, mini size
1/2 cup grated cheese
2 tablespoons fresh
 mint leaves, extra

1. Place chicken in food
processor. Process
20–30 seconds or until
finely minced. Heat oil
in large frying pan; add
garlic, onion and leek.
Cook over medium
heat 5–10 minutes or
until soft and golden.

Hawaiian Teriyaki Burger (top) and Chicken Sloppy Joe.

Increase heat; add sliced mushrooms. Cook mushrooms 2–3 minutes or until soft. Stir in paprika, salt, pepper and chicken. Continue to cook over medium heat 5–6 minutes, stirring to break up any lumps as the chicken cooks.

2. Add flour, cook 1 minute. Gradually add milk, stirring continually, and cook until mixture boils and thickens. Add creamed corn, mint and chilli sauce. Stir until mixture is heated through. Reduce heat to low; keep warm.

3. Place pizza bases on cold grill tray. Toast each side lightly under preheated grill. Sprinkle each with cheese, grill until cheese has melted. Place pizza bases on 4 serving plates. Spread chicken mixture on each and top with extra mint leaves.

Chicken Cordon Bleu Burger

Preparation time:
 30 minutes
Total cooking time:
 10 minutes
Serves 4

4 chicken breast fillets
4 slices ham
3/4 cup grated cheddar
 or gruyére cheese
1/4 cup thinly sliced
 fresh basil
salt and pepper
plain flour
2 eggs, lightly beaten
oil
1 teaspoon English or
 Australian mustard
1/3 cup whole egg
 mayonnaise
1 teaspoon lemon juice
1 tank loaf, cut into
 8 slices
lettuce
8 canned artichoke
 hearts, drained, sliced

1. Trim chicken of excess fat. Cut into thickest section of each fillet horizontally without cutting right through. Open fillet out.
2. Place a slice of ham on one side of each fillet. Top with cheese and basil, season with salt and pepper. Fold remaining half of fillet over to enclose filling. Coat each fillet with flour. Dip into egg and coat again with flour.
3. Heat oil in pan; add chicken. Cook over medium heat 3–4 minutes each side or until cooked through.
4. Mix mustard, mayonnaise and juice in bowl. Toast bread. Place 4 slices on serving plates. On each slice, place lettuce and fillets. Spoon over mayonnaise mixture, followed by artichoke slices and toast.

Chicken Cordon Bleu Burger.

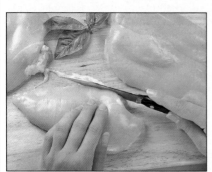

1. Using a sharp knife, trim chicken fillets of excess fat and sinew.

2. Place a slice of ham on one side of each fillet. Top with cheese and basil.

32

3. Cook coated fillets in oil until each side is golden and chicken is cooked.

4. Combine mustard, mayonnaise and lemon juice in a small bowl and mix well.

Apricot Veal Burger with Yoghurt Dressing

Preparation time:
  30 minutes
Total cooking time:
  10–15 minutes
Serves 4

Yoghurt dressing
1/4 cup plain yoghurt
2–3 teaspoons honey
1–2 teaspoons tahini or
  peanut butter
1 clove garlic extra,
  crushed

500 g pork and veal
  mince
1/4 cup finely chopped
  dried apricots
4 spring onions, finely
  chopped
2 teaspoons sweet chilli
  sauce
1 clove garlic, crushed
salt and pepper
1 egg, lightly beaten
1–2 tablespoons fresh
  white breadcrumbs
1 large red capsicum
oil for frying
1 focaccia, cut into
  quarters
snow pea sprouts for
  serving

**1. To make yoghurt
dressing:** Combine
yoghurt, honey, tahini
or peanut butter and
garlic in small bowl,
mix well.
2. Combine mince,

apricots, spring onions,
chilli sauce, garlic, salt,
pepper, egg and
breadcrumbs in large
bowl. Mix with hands
until well combined.
Divide mixture into
4 and shape into round
patties; cover and
refrigerate 10 minutes.
3. Cut capsicum in half.
Remove seeds and
membrane. Place
capsicum, skin side up
on grill tray and brush
lightly with oil. Cook
under preheated grill
4–5 minutes or until
skin has blistered and
black. Remove from
heat, cover with a damp
tea-towel until cool.
Peel away skin and cut
into thin strips.
4. Heat oil in large
heavy-based frying pan.
Cook patties over
medium heat 3–4
minutes each side or
until brown and cooked
through. Drain on
paper towels. Slice
focaccia in half
horizontally. Lightly
toast cut sides and
butter if desired. Place
bases on serving plates;
on each, place sprouts, a
patty, capsicum strips,
yoghurt dressing and a
final slice of focaccia.

Chicken Schnitzel Burger

Preparation time:
  20 minutes
Total cooking time:
  5–10 minutes
Serves 4

4 chicken breast fillets
1 egg
2 tablespoons milk
2/3 cup breadcrumbs
1 tablespoon fresh
  chopped chives
2 teaspoons fresh
  chopped parsley
2 tablespoons ground
  walnuts
plain flour
salt and pepper
30 g butter
1 tablespoon olive oil
4 fancy bread rolls
salad mix (mesclun) for
  serving
green mango chutney
  for serving

1. Trim chicken of
excess fat and sinew.
Place chicken fillets
between two sheets of
plastic wrap, flatten
using a meat mallet or a
rolling pin. In a small
bowl, beat egg and
milk. Combine the
breadcrumbs, chives,
parsley and walnuts on
a plate. Dust chicken in
seasoned flour; shake
off excess. Dip chicken
in egg mixture and
coat well with
breadcrumb mixture.

Chicken Schnitzel Burger (left) and Apricot Veal Burger with Yoghurt Dressing.

2. Heat butter and oil in large heavy-based frying pan. Cook chicken schnitzels in batches over medium heat 2–3 minutes each side or until golden brown and cooked through. Remove schnitzels from pan and drain on paper towels.

3. Cut bread rolls in half. Lightly toast the cut sides and butter if desired. Place roll bases on 4 serving plates. On each base, place salad mix and a schnitzel. Top with a spoonful of green mango chutney if desired. Finish with the top half of bread roll.

Note: May be served with mayonnaise or mustard instead of green mango chutney.

35

Asian Chicken Burger

Preparation time:
20 minutes
Total cooking time:
15 minutes
Serves 4

2 tablespoons peanut oil
1 onion, finely chopped
2 teaspoons grated
  fresh ginger
2 cloves garlic, crushed
500 g chicken fillets,
  chopped
1–2 tablespoons soy
  sauce
1 tablespoon rice wine
1 tablespoon hoisin
  sauce
2 teaspoons sugar
1/3 cup finely chopped
  water chestnuts
extra oil for frying
200 g bean sprouts
1 tablespoon sesame
  seeds
pepper to taste
2 cups shredded
  Chinese cabbage
1 teaspoon soy sauce,
  extra
4 damper rolls
sour cream, optional

1. Heat peanut oil in
medium pan; add
onion, ginger and
garlic. Cook over
medium heat 2–3
minutes or until soft.
Remove from heat and
allow to cool.
2. Process chicken in
food processor 15–20
seconds or until minced.
Transfer chicken to
mixing bowl, add onion
mixture, soy sauce, rice
wine, hoisin sauce, sugar
and water chestnuts;
mix well. Divide
mixture into 4 portions
and shape into patties.
3. Heat a little oil in
frying pan. Cook patties
over medium heat for
3–4 minutes each side
or until brown and
cooked through.
Remove from pan;
keep warm. Add bean
sprouts, sesame seeds,
pepper, cabbage and
extra soy sauce to pan.
Stir-fry 2–3 minutes or
until heated through.
4. Cut rolls in half
horizontally. Place roll
bases on serving plates.
On each base place some
cabbage mixture and
a patty. Add sour cream
if desired. Finish with a
roll top.

Cracked Wheat and Lamb Burger

Preparation time:
25 minutes + standing
Total cooking time:
5–10 minutes
Serves 4

1/4 cup cracked wheat
  (burghul)
1/4 cup water
400 g lean lamb mince
1 tablespoon lemon
  juice
1/3 cup finely chopped
  parsley
2 cloves garlic, crushed
2 tablespoons chopped
  fresh mint
1/2 teaspoon salt
1/2 teaspoon coarsely
  ground black pepper
2–3 tablespoons oil
1 large red onion, finely
  chopped
1 large tomato, finely
  chopped
1 clove garlic, crushed
2 teaspoons chopped
  fresh mint, extra
salt and pepper
  to taste
1 teaspoon soft brown
  sugar
4 wholegrain rolls
curly endive
plain yoghurt for
  serving, optional

1. Place cracked wheat
and water in medium
bowl and allow to
stand for 30 minutes.
Drain and squeeze out
excess water. Combine
with lamb mince,
lemon juice, parsley,
garlic, mint, salt and
pepper. Mix with
hands until well
combined. Divide
mixture into 4 portions
and shape into patties.
2. Heat oil in large
frying pan. Add patties,
cook over medium heat

Cracked Wheat and Lamb Burger (top) and Asian Chicken Burger.

3–4 minutes each side or until brown and cooked through.
3. Combine onion, tomato, garlic, mint, salt, pepper and sugar in small bowl. Mix well. Cut rolls in half horizontally. Place roll bases on 4 serving plates. On each base place endive, a patty, onion mixture and finally a roll top. May be served with a dollop of yoghurt, and side dishes of crispy potato or pumpkin curls.

37

Sesame Pork Burger

Preparation time:
30 minutes
Total cooking time:
10–15 minutes
Serves 4

375 g lean pork mince
2 teaspoons fresh
  grated ginger
2 cloves garlic,
  crushed
*1/3 cup chopped water
  chestnuts*
*1/2 cup finely grated
  carrot*
*1/2 cup finely shredded
  Chinese cabbage*
1 tablespoon soy sauce
1 tablespoon sweet
  chilli sauce
1 teaspoon sugar
salt and pepper
1 tablespoon peanut oil
1 tablespoon sesame oil
1 cup bean sprouts
1 zucchini, thinly sliced
  diagonally
1/2 cup shredded rocket
60 g snow pea sprouts
4 knot rolls

1. Combine mince,
ginger, garlic, water
chestnuts, carrot,
cabbage, soy sauce, chilli
sauce, sugar, salt and
pepper. Mix with hands
until well combined.
Divide mixture into
4 equal portions;
shape into patties.

2. Heat peanut oil in
frying pan. Cook
patties over medium
heat 3–4 minutes each
side or until brown and
cooked through.
Remove from pan; keep
warm. Heat sesame oil
in pan; add bean
sprouts, zucchini,
rocket and snow pea
sprouts. Toss vegetables
over medium heat
2–3 minutes until
heated through.
3. Cut rolls in half
horizontally. Lightly
toast cut sides and
butter if desired. Place
roll bases on 4 serving
plates. On each base,
place a meat patty
followed by vegetable
mixture and a roll top.

Pork and Apple Burger

Preparation time:
25 minutes
Total cooking time:
15–20 minutes
Serves 4

4 pitted prunes, halved
4 pork butterfly steaks
1 tablespoon mild
  American mustard
1/4 cup thick cream
salt and pepper
2 medium unpeeled
  green apples
30 g butter
1 tablespoon oil
1 clove garlic, crushed
1 tank loaf
80 g snow pea sprouts

1. Place prunes in
medium bowl. Cover
with boiling water and
leave to stand. Trim
pork of excess fat and
sinew. Combine
mustard, cream, salt
and pepper in small
bowl; set aside.
2. Using an apple corer,
remove core from
apples. Cut apples in
1 cm thick rings. Heat
butter in large frying
pan. Add apple rings,
cook over medium heat
2–3 minutes each side
or until tender. Remove
from pan, keep warm.
Add oil and garlic to
pan, cook 1 minute.
Add pork steaks, cook
2–3 minutes each side
or until lightly browned
and cooked through.
3. Drain prunes well.
Using a sharp serrated
knife, cut tank loaf into
8 equal slices. Lightly
toast each side and
spread with butter if
desired. Place 4 slices
on serving plates. On
each slice, place snow
pea sprouts, steak,
apple, prunes, mustard
mixture. Top with
another slice of toast.

---

*Sesame Pork Burger (top) and
Pork and Apple Burger.*

Paprika Chicken and Potato Burger

Preparation time:
20–30 minutes
Total cooking time:
20 minutes
Serves 4

2 tablespoons olive oil
1 medium onion, finely
chopped
500 g lean chicken
mince
2 teaspoons paprika
1/4 teaspoon chilli
powder
1/2 cup fresh white
breadcrumbs
1/4 cup sour cream
1 teaspoon salt
1/2 teaspoon white
pepper
oil for frying
2 large new potatoes,
sliced very thinly
8 thick slices baguette
loaf
1 small green
capsicum, sliced in
thin rounds

bread and butter
cucumbers, drained
whole egg mayonnaise

1. Heat oil in small
pan. Add onion, cook
over medium heat 3–4
minutes or until soft
and golden. Remove
from heat; cool slightly.
Combine chicken
mince, paprika, chilli,
breadcrumbs, cream,
salt, pepper and onion
in large bowl. Mix with
hands until well
combined. Divide
mixture into 4 portions
and shape into
round patties.
2. Pour oil into
medium pan to depth
of 2 cm and heat to
moderately hot. Pat
potato slices dry with
paper towels. Cook
potato slices in small
batches 2–3 minutes or
until they turn golden.
Drain on paper towels.
Cover and keep warm.

3. Heat a large frying
pan or grill plate, brush
liberally with oil. Cook
patties 3–4 minutes
each side or until golden
and cooked through.
4. Toast baguette slices
and butter if desired. On
4 slices of toast, overlap
cooked potato slices.
Add slices of capsicum
and a patty, cucumbers
and mayonnaise. Top
with a slice of toast.
Garnish with fresh
herbs, if desired.

HINT
Chicken mince is
available from your
butcher or chicken
shop. If you prefer,
you can make it in a
food processor. Buy
skinless thigh or
breast fillets, trim
off all excess fat, cut
into cubes and
process in batches
until finely minced.

Paprika Chicken and Potato Burger.

1. Using your hands, divide mixture into
4 portions and shape into round patties.

2. Cook potato slices in small batches.
Remove with slotted spatula. Drain.

3. Cook patties for 3–4 minutes on each side or until golden and cooked through.

4. Place patties over slices of potato and green capsicum. Add cucumbers.

Egg and Bacon Breakfast Burger

Preparation time:
15–20 minutes
Total cooking time:
5–10 minutes
Serves 4

oil for frying
4 thick bacon rashers,
  each cut into 4,
  rind removed
4 eggs
8 waffles
4 slices cheddar cheese
maple syrup, optional

1. Heat a small amount of oil in frying pan. Fry bacon and eggs over medium heat until eggs are cooked through and bacon rashers are golden and crisp.
2. While eggs and bacon are cooking, lightly toast waffles on both sides. Place cheese slices on 4 waffles and cook under preheated grill 1–2 minutes or until cheese has melted. Place on individual serving plates.
3. Place egg and bacon on each waffle. Drizzle maple syrup over, if desired. Top with remaining waffle and serve immediately. If preferred, drizzle with worcestershire sauce.

Pork and Peanut Burger with Minted Cabbage

Preparation time:
35 minutes
Total cooking time:
5–10 minutes
Serves 4

2 cups finely shredded
  cabbage
1 small red onion,
  finely chopped
1 small carrot, finely
  grated
1 tablespoon chopped
  fresh mint
1/4 cup finely chopped
  fresh or canned
  pineapple
1/4 cup whole egg
  mayonnaise
1 stick celery, finely
  chopped
2 teaspoons orange or
  lemon juice
375 g lean pork mince
1 tablespoon crunchy
  peanut butter
1/4 cup cooked white rice
2 spring onions, finely
  sliced
1 tablespoon lemon
  juice
1 clove garlic, crushed
1 egg
2–3 tablespoons finely
  chopped honey
  roasted peanuts
salt and ground black
  pepper to taste
4 damper rolls
Apple, apricot and nut
  chutney (see page 63),
  optional

1. Combine shredded cabbage, red onion, carrot, mint, pineapple, mayonnaise, celery and juice in medium bowl; mix well. Set aside.
2. Combine mince, peanut butter, rice, spring onion, lemon juice, garlic, egg, peanuts, salt and pepper in medium bowl. Mix with hands until well combined. Divide mixture into 4 portions, shape each into round patties.
3. Heat a large frying pan or grill plate, brush with oil. Cook patties 3–4 minutes each side or until brown and cooked through. Halve damper rolls horizontally. Lightly toast and butter if desired. Place roll bases on 4 serving plates. Spoon some drained cabbage mixture onto each base. Add a meat patty and a spoonful of chutney, if desired. Place a roll top on each.

Pork and Peanut Burger with Minted Cabbage (top) and Egg and Bacon Breakfast Burger.

Sausage and Cheese Burger

Preparation time:
20 minutes
Total cooking time:
5–10 minutes
Serves 4

4 thick pork sausages
1/4 cup tomato relish or
 chutney
1 tablespoon
 wholegrain mustard
1/2 cup grated cheddar
 cheese
8 slices white bread or
 8 square crumpets
1 tomato, thinly sliced
green oak leaf lettuce
black pepper, optional

1. Cut each sausage
down the centre
lengthways, three-
quarters of the way
through. Open sausage
out, placing cut side
down. Make small
diagonal slashes along
each sausage. (This will
prevent the sausage from
curling while cooking.)
2. Heat a grill plate,
brush liberally with oil.
Cook sausages 2–3
minutes each side or
until brown and
cooked through. Place
sausages cut side down
on foil-lined tray. Top
each sausage with
combined relish or
chutney and mustard.
Sprinkle with cheese.
Cook under preheated

grill 1–2 minutes or
until cheese has melted.
3. Lightly toast bread
or crumpets on each
side and spread with
butter if desired. On
4 of them place tomato
slices, lettuce and a
cooked sausage (cheese
side up). Sprinkle with
pepper if desired and
serve with remaining
toast or crumpets.

Herb Burger

Preparation time:
20 minutes +
refrigeration
Total cooking time:
10–15 minutes
Serves 4

250 g lean beef mince
250 g pork mince
2 tablespoons finely
 chopped parsley
2 teaspoons finely
 chopped fresh thyme
 or 3/4 teaspoon dried
2 teaspoons finely
 chopped fresh
 rosemary or
 3/4 teaspoon dried
1 teaspoon finely
 chopped fresh
 marjoram or
 1/2 teaspoon dried

1 teaspoon finely grated
 lemon rind
3/4 teaspoon salt
1/2 teaspoon black
 pepper
1 clove garlic, crushed
1/4 cup red wine
1 tablespoon oil
20 g butter
3 teaspoons soft brown
 sugar
1 large firm ripe
 mango, peeled and
 thinly sliced
4 cornmeal rolls
red and green coral
 lettuce leaves
relish, optional

1. Combine beef mince,
pork mince, parsley,
thyme, rosemary,
marjoram, lemon rind,
salt, pepper, crushed
garlic and red wine in
large bowl. Mix with
hands until well
combined. Divide
mixture into 4 portions
and shape into round
patties. Cover and
refrigerate for
30 minutes or for
up to 12 hours.
2. Heat oil in large
frying pan. Cook
patties over medium
heat 3–4 minutes each
side or until brown and
cooked through. While
patties are cooking,
heat butter in small
shallow frying pan.
Add soft brown sugar,
stir over low heat until
sugar is dissolved. Add
the mango slices and
simmer 2–3 minutes

Sausage and Cheese Burger (top) and Herb Burger.

each side or until well coated and a light brown in colour. (Do not allow the mango to become too soft.)

3. Cut cornmeal rolls in half horizontally and toast cut sides if desired. Place roll bases on 4 serving plates. On each base, place lettuce leaves, a meat patty and some mango slices. Add a spoonful of relish, if desired. Finish each burger with a roll top.

45

Italian Salami Burger

Preparation time:
  20 minutes
Total cooking time:
  20 minutes
Serves 4

80 g butter, softened
¹/2 teaspoon ground
  black pepper
1–2 cloves garlic, crushed
2 green capsicum
4 round wholemeal
  focaccia rolls
2 tomatoes, sliced
8 large round slices
  spicy salami
3 spring onions, sliced
¹/3 cup parmesan
  cheese shavings

1. Preheat oven to moderate 180°C. Beat butter, pepper and garlic in small bowl until smooth. Cut capsicum in half, remove seeds and membrane. Place skin side up on cold grill tray. Brush skin with oil. Cook under preheated grill until skin is black. Remove; cover with damp tea-towel until cooled. Peel away skin. Cut capsicum flesh in 2 cm strips.
2. Cut rolls in half horizontally. Spread cut sides with butter mixture. Place focaccia bases onto foil-lined oven tray. On each base, place tomato slices, two slices of salami, capsicum, spring onion, cheese and finally a roll top. Bake in oven for 15 minutes. May be served with hot potato skins.

Ham and Pineapple Burger

Preparation time:
  25 minutes
Total cooking time:
  5–10 minutes
Serves 4

1 cup finely shredded
  cabbage
3 spring onions, finely
  sliced
1 medium carrot,
  grated
2 tablespoons whole
  egg mayonnaise
1 teaspoon lemon or
  lime juice
1 teaspoon grated
  lemon or lime rind
4 slices canned
  pineapple, juice
  reserved
1 tablespoon honey
2 teaspoons grated
  fresh ginger
1 tablespoon lemon or
  lime juice, extra
1 teaspoon mustard
  powder
1 teaspoon soft brown
  sugar
4 large ham steaks
  (1.25 cm thick)
4 flat bread rolls

1. Combine cabbage, onion, carrot, mayonnaise and lemon or lime juice in a bowl; mix well. Set aside.
2. Place rind, ¹/2 cup pineapple juice, honey, ginger, extra juice, mustard and sugar in large frying pan. Bring mixture to boil, add ham steaks. Cook steaks over medium heat 3–4 minutes or until all liquid is absorbed and steaks have a glazed coating. Move steaks to one side of the pan. Add pineapple rings, cook until heated through, turning once.
3. Halve bread rolls and lightly toast each side; spread with butter if desired. Place roll bases on serving plates. On each base, place a ham steak followed by pineapple and drained cabbage mixture. Finish with a roll top.

Ham and Pineapple Burger (top) and
Italian Salami Burger.

Super Cheese Burger

Preparation time:
20–30 minutes
Total cooking time:
15 minutes
Serves 4

750 g lean beef mince
1 small onion, finely
  chopped
1 tablespoon tomato
  paste
1 tablespoon fresh
  chopped chives
2 tablespoons finely
  grated parmesan
  cheese
salt and pepper
50 g vintage cheddar
  cheese
40 g cream cheese
1–2 tablespoons sour
  cream
2 tablespoons finely
  grated smoked cheese
1 teaspoon grated
  lemon rind
4 crusty wholegrain
  rolls
butter lettuce
fresh thyme, chopped
vegetables for serving,
  optional

1. Combine mince,
onion, tomato paste,
chives, parmesan
cheese, salt and pepper
in large bowl. Mix with
hands until well
combined. Divide
mixture into
4 portions. Cut cheddar
cheese into 4 squares
about 2–3cm wide and
1 cm thick. Place a
square of cheese in the
centre of each mince
portion. Smooth mince
around the cheese to
enclose it. Shape mince
into a round patty.
2. Heat a large frying
pan or grill plate, brush
liberally with oil. Cook
patties 6–7 minutes
each side or until
brown and cooked
through. While patties
are cooking, beat cream
cheese with electric
beaters until smooth.
Add sour cream,
smoked cheese and
lemon rind, beat until
well combined.
3. Cut rolls in half
horizontally. Lightly
toast cut sides under
preheated grill and
place roll bases on
4 serving plates. On
each base, place lettuce,
a meat patty and a
dollop of cream cheese
mixture. Sprinkle with
thyme and finish with a
roll top. May be served
with mixed grilled
vegetables, if desired.

HINT
It is better to buy
parmesan cheese in
a block and grate it
yourself. The
flavour is superior
to the parmesan
cheese that is
available already
grated in packets.

Fresh Salmon Burger

Preparation time:
25 minutes + standing
Total cooking time:
10–12 minutes
Serves 4

400 g fresh salmon
  fillet
2 tablespoons lemon
  juice
1/2 teaspoon cracked
  black pepper
2 Lebanese cucumbers,
  thinly sliced
1 teaspoon salt
1 teaspoon sugar
2 tablespoons French
  mustard
2 teaspoons hot English
  mustard
2 tablespoons sour
  cream
2 teaspoons lemon
  juice, extra
2 tablespoons light
  olive oil
1 leek, finely sliced
4 white bagels, halved
4 coral lettuce leaves
1 hard-boiled egg,
  sliced
black caviar

1. Cut salmon into
4 pieces. Sprinkle with
lemon juice, season
with pepper. Place
cucumber, salt and
sugar in small bowl;
stand 20 minutes, drain.
Combine mustards,
sour cream and extra
juice in a small jug.

Super Cheese Burger (top) and Fresh Salmon Burger.

2. Heat 1 tablespoon oil in large frying pan. Add salmon, cook over high heat 1 minute on each side. Cover, remove from heat and leave for 3 minutes to cook through.

3. Heat remaining oil in frying pan. Cook leek 4–5 minutes or until soft.
4. Place bagel bases on 4 serving plates. On each base, place lettuce, drained cucumber and

a piece of salmon, followed by mustard mixture, leek, egg, $1/2$ teaspoon caviar, and a bagel top. Garnish with sprigs of dill, if desired. May be served with crisp potato slices.

Mushroom and Pine Nut Burger

Preparation time:
40 minutes +
refrigeration
Total cooking time:
15–20 minutes
Serves 4

4 tablespoons light
olive oil
1 onion, finely
chopped
1 clove garlic, finely
chopped
375 g mushrooms,
cut into thick slices
1 egg
1 cup fresh
breadcrumbs
1/3 cup pine nuts,
toasted
3 teaspoons finely
chopped fresh thyme
1 teaspoon salt
1/2 teaspoon pepper
1/2 red capsicum, sliced
into strips lengthways
1 cup grated carrot
2 spring onions, finely
sliced
1/4 teaspoon Tabasco
2 tablespoons
mayonnaise
2 tablespoons sour
cream
4 crusty white rolls
shredded lettuce
50 g parmesan cheese,
shaved

1. Heat 2 tablespoons
oil in large frying pan.
Add chopped onion
and garlic, cook until

soft, about 10 minutes.
Add sliced mushrooms,
cook over high heat
until they have become
tender and all moisture
has evaporated.
Remove from heat and
allow to cool.
2. Place mushroom
mixture in food
processor and puree
with egg and
breadcrumbs. Stir in
pine nuts, thyme, salt
and pepper. Refrigerate
for several hours or
until firm. Divide into
4 portions and shape
into patties with wet
hands. Heat remaining
oil in frying pan, cook
patties over medium
heat 3–4 minutes each
side until brown.
Remove patties from
frying pan and keep
warm. Add capsicum
and cook 3 minutes
or until soft.
3. In a small bowl,
combine grated carrot,
spring onion, Tabasco,
mayonnaise and the
sour cream.
4. Cut rolls in half
horizontally and toast
cut sides. Place roll
bases on 4 serving
plates. Spread carrot
mixture evenly over
each base, followed by
lettuce and a patty.
Add strips of capsicum
and large shavings of
parmesan cheese.
Finish by placing
remaining roll half
on top.

Crab Cake Burger with Chilli Cream

Preparation time:
25 minutes
Total cooking time:
5–10 minutes
Serves 4

Chilli Cream
1/4 cup sour cream
2–3 teaspoons sweet or
hot chilli sauce
1/2 teaspoon ground
cumin
1 tablespoon plain
yoghurt
2 teaspoons fresh
chopped chives

200 g crab meat,
drained
1 cup fresh breadcrumbs
2 spring onions, finely
chopped
1/4 cup whole egg
mayonnaise
1 tablespoon lime juice
1 tablespoon chopped
fresh coriander
1 tablespoon finely
chopped red capsicum
1 egg, lightly beaten
1/2 teaspoon grated
lime rind
salt and pepper to taste
oil for shallow frying
1 round Italian crusty
loaf, quartered
cos lettuce leaves

**1. *To make chilli
cream:*** Combine all
chilli cream ingredients
in a small bowl. Stir
until combined.

Mushroom and Pine Nut Burger (top) and Crab Cake Burger with Chilli Cream.

2. In a bowl, mix crab meat, breadcrumbs, onion, mayonnaise, juice, coriander, capsicum, egg, rind, salt and pepper. Divide mixture into 4 portions.

3. Heat oil in frying pan. Drop each crab portion into pan, cook over medium heat 2–3 minutes each side; remove crab cake, drain on paper towels.

4. Halve bread quarters horizontally. Toast each side. Place bread bases on 4 serving plates and, on each place lettuce, crab cake, chilli cream and top quarter of bread.

51

1. *Combine beef and sausage mince, egg, salt, pepper and breadcrumbs in a bowl.*

2. *Add mustard to pan and cook mixture, stirring, for 2 minutes.*

Tomato and Olive Burger Roll

Preparation time:
20 minutes
Total cooking time:
15–20 minutes
Serves 4

500 g lean beef mince
200 g sausage mince
1 egg
2 teaspoons finely
  chopped fresh oregano
  or ¹/2 teaspoon dried
¹/4 teaspoon salt
¹/4 teaspoon cracked
  black pepper
2 tablespoons dried
  breadcrumbs
30 g butter
1 onion, finely sliced
10 cherry tomatoes,
  halved
10 stuffed green olives,
  sliced
¹/2 cup tomato sauce
2–3 teaspoons
  horseradish
1 teaspoon
  worcestershire sauce
1 tablespoon French or
  German mustard
4 slices lavash bread

1. Combine beef and sausage mince, egg, oregano, salt, pepper and breadcrumbs in large bowl. Mix with hands until well combined. Divide mixture into 4. Roll each portion into a long sausage shape. Cover and set aside.
2. Heat butter in medium pan. Add onion, cook over medium heat until onion is golden and soft. Add tomatoes, olives, tomato sauce, horseradish, worcestershire sauce and mustard. Cook, stirring, for 2 minutes. Bring to boil, reduce heat; simmer uncovered 5–10 minutes or until liquid reduces and sauce thickens. Remove pan from heat.
3. Heat a small amount of oil in large frying pan. Cook burgers 6–8 minutes over medium heat, turning regularly to ensure even cooking and browning. Remove from heat. Drain on paper towels.
4. Place burgers on lavash bread diagonally across one corner. Spoon tomato and olive mixture over burger. Fold three nearest ends over mixture and roll up into a parcel. Fold firmly to stop the filling from falling out.

> HINT
> Canned tomatoes, drained and chopped, can be substituted for cherry tomatoes. Try to use fresh tomatoes, however, as they do give a better flavour.

Tomato and Olive Burger Roll.

3. Cook burgers over medium heat turning regularly. Drain on paper towels.

4. Fold ends firmly over filling and roll up into a parcel.

Chick Pea and Vegetable Burger with Hummus

Preparation time:
20–30minutes +
2 hours refrigeration
Total cooking time:
15–20 minutes
Serves 4

Hummus
310 g can chick peas, drained
2 cloves garlic, crushed
2 tablespoons lemon juice
2 tablespoons sour cream
1 tablespoon peanut butter or tahini
1 teaspoon ground cumin
2 tablespoons toasted sesame seeds

1/2 cup olive oil
1 medium onion, finely chopped
1 tablespoon curry powder
1/2 cup fresh or frozen peas
1/2 cup finely chopped carrot
1/2 cup finely chopped pumpkin
1 tomato, peeled and chopped
3/4 cup fresh white breadcrumbs
1 egg
salt and pepper

310 g chick peas, extra, drained
1 rye loaf, sliced
lettuce
1 Lebanese cucumber, thinly sliced lengthways
1 tomato, extra, thinly sliced
1 red onion, cut in thin slices

1. **To make hummus:**
Place chick peas, garlic, juice, cream, peanut butter, cumin and sesame seeds in food processor. Process 20–30 seconds or until smooth. Set aside.
2. Heat 2 tablespoons oil in medium pan; add onion and curry powder. Cook over medium heat 3–4 minutes or until softened. Stir in peas, carrot and pumpkin; cook 2 minutes. Add tomato, reduce heat, cover and cook 3–5 minutes or until vegetables are soft. Remove from heat, cool slightly. Stir in crumbs, egg, salt and pepper. Transfer to a bowl.
3. Place extra chick peas in food processor. Process until smooth. Add to vegetable mixture and mix well. Cover, refrigerate 2 hours. Divide the mixture into 4 portions. Shape each into flat round patties.
4. Heat remaining oil in frying pan. Cook patties

over medium heat 3–4 minutes each side or until golden and cooked through. Lightly toast bread, if desired. Place 4 bread slices on serving plates. On each slice, place lettuce, cucumber, tomato, onion slices and a patty. Spoon hummus over patty and finish with another slice of toast.

Herb and Onion Burger

Preparation time:
20 minutes
Total cooking time:
10 minutes
Serves 4

400 g lean beef mince
350 g pork and veal mince
1/4 teaspoon salt
1/4 teaspoon white pepper
1 tablespoon barbecue sauce
1 small red onion, finely chopped
1 teaspoon dried mixed herbs
1 teaspoon chopped fresh mint
30 g butter
6 large spring onions, diagonally sliced

Herb and Onion Burger (top) and Chick Pea and Vegetable Burger with Hummus.

4 crusty rolls, halved
curly endive or mizuna
sauce or relish
125 g camembert
  cheese, thinly sliced

1. Combine beef mince, pork and veal mince, salt, pepper, sauce, onion, herbs and mint in large bowl. Mix with hands until well combined. Divide mixture into 4 portions and shape into patties.
2. Heat a large frying pan or grill plate, brush liberally with oil. Cook patties 3–4 minutes each side or until brown and cooked through. When patties are almost cooked, heat butter in a pan. Add onion, cook until soft.
3. Toast cut sides of rolls, and butter. Place bases on 4 serving plates. On each base, place curly endive, a meat patty, relish, cheese, onion and finally a roll top.

55

Chilli Burger

Preparation time:
20 minutes
Total cooking time:
10–15 minutes
Serves 4

500 g lean beef mince
4 spring onions, finely
chopped
2 tablespoons sweet
chilli sauce
1 clove garlic, crushed
2 teaspoons
worcestershire sauce
1 tablespoon tomato
paste
2 tablespoons chopped
fresh coriander
salt and pepper
Tabasco to taste
1 large red onion, cut in
1 cm rings
1/4 cup soy sauce
3 teaspoons soft brown
sugar
lettuce leaves
8 thick slices Vienna
loaf
4 jalapeno chillies,
finely sliced

1. Combine mince,
onion, chilli sauce,
garlic, worcestershire
sauce, tomato paste,
coriander, salt, pepper
and Tabasco in a large
bowl. Mix with hands
until well combined.
Divide mixture into
4 portions and shape
into patties.
2. Heat a large frying
pan or grill plate, brush
liberally with oil. Cook
patties 3–4 minutes
each side or until
brown and cooked
through. While patties
are cooking, cook
whole onion rings,
brushing with
combined soy sauce
and sugar until onion
is just tender.
3. Wash and pat dry
lettuce leaves with
paper towel. Toast
bread and place 4 slices
on serving plates. On
each slice, place lettuce,
a meat patty, onion
rings and jalapeno
chilli followed by
another slice of toast.
May be served with
potato wedges.

Vegetarian Burger

Preparation time:
25 minutes
Total cooking time:
10 minutes
Serves 4

400 g silken tofu,
drained
1 medium carrot, peeled
1 punnet fresh baby
corn
1/4 cup peanut oil
1 medium onion, thinly
sliced
1 clove garlic, crushed
1 stalk celery, finely
sliced
1 red capsicum, cut in
thin strips
1/4 cup water
2 teaspoons cornflour
1 tablespoon sweet
chilli sauce
2 teaspoons soy sauce
2 tablespoons
cornflour, extra
1 teaspoon ground
paprika
1 teaspoon ground
turmeric
1 teaspoon ground
coriander
1 loaf of rye bread,
sliced and toasted
alfalfa sprouts

1. Cut tofu into eight
slices; drain on paper
towels. Using a
vegetable peeler,
peel the carrot into
long ribbons. Cut corn
in half lengthways.
2. Heat half the oil in
a large frying pan or
wok. Add onion and
garlic, cook over
medium heat 1 minute.
Stir in carrot, celery,
capsicum and corn.
Stir-fry over medium-
high heat 2–3 minutes.
Add blended water,
cornflour, chilli sauce
and soy sauce. Cook
1–2 more minutes or
until mixture boils and
thickens and vegetables
are just tender. Remove
from heat, keep warm.
3. Combine extra
cornflour, paprika,
turmeric and coriander
on sheet of greaseproof
paper. Carefully coat
drained tofu slices
with mixture. Heat
remaining oil in

Vegetarian Burger (top) and Chilli Burger.

medium frying pan. Add tofu slices and cook over medium heat 1–2 minutes each side or until golden. Drain on paper towels.

4. Place 4 slices of toasted rye bread onto individual serving plates. On each slice of bread, place alfalfa sprouts (or a lettuce leaf, if preferred), some of the vegetable mixture, and 2 slices of fried tofu. Finish with another slice of toasted rye bread.

Condiments

Making chutneys and sauces is a traditional and delicious way of preserving fruit and vegetables.

Spicy Barbecue Sauce

Preparation time:
  35 minutes + standing
Total cooking time:
  1¹/2–2 hours
Makes about 7 cups

2 large red capsicum,
  seeds and membrane
  removed, roughly
  chopped
2 kg ripe tomatoes,
  roughly chopped
3 medium onions,
  finely chopped
3 sticks celery, finely
  chopped
2¹/2 cups malt vinegar
2 red chillies, finely
  chopped
3 cloves garlic, crushed
2 teaspoons grated
  fresh ginger
1 tablespoon fresh
  coriander leaves,
  shredded
1 teaspoon ground
  cumin
1 teaspoon mixed spice
2 teaspoons cracked
  black pepper

1 teaspoon hot English
  mustard
2 tablespoons paprika
1 teaspoon Tabasco
1¹/2 cups soft brown
  sugar

1. Combine capsicum, tomato, onion, celery, vinegar, chillies, garlic, ginger, coriander, cumin, spice, pepper, mustard, paprika and Tabasco in a large heavy-based pan. Bring to the boil, stirring occasionally over medium heat. Reduce heat and simmer uncovered for 1 hour.
2. Cool slightly for about 15 minutes, pour into food processor and puree. Return mixture to pan. Add sugar and stir over low heat until sugar is dissolved. Simmer for 30 minutes or until mixture is thick enough to coat the back of a spoon.
3. Pour mixture into hot sterilised jars; seal immediately. Leave 2 days before using.

Ginger Peach Relish (left) and Spicy Barbecue Sauce.

Ginger Peach Relish

Preparation time:
15 minutes + standing
Total cooking time:
20–25 minutes
Makes about 4 cups

6 large ripe peaches, peeled
1 tablespoon finely chopped preserved ginger in syrup
2 tablespoons soft brown sugar
2 spring onions, finely chopped
1/4 teaspoon mixed spice
2 whole cloves
4 whole black peppercorns
2 tablespoons brown vinegar
2 teaspoons soy sauce

1. Cut peaches in half and remove stones. Roughly chop flesh.
2. Combine peaches, ginger, sugar, onions, spice, cloves, peppercorns, vinegar and soy sauce in large heavy-based pan. Stir over medium heat until sugar dissolves. Bring mixture to boil, reduce heat and simmer, covered, for 15 minutes or until mixture has become soft and pulpy. Remove pan from heat and discard cloves and peppercorns.

3. Spoon mixture into warm sterilised jars and seal. When cool, label and date jars. Keep refrigerated until required but leave 2 days before opening.

Old-Fashioned Bread and Butter Cucumbers

Preparation time:
40 minutes + standing
Total cooking time:
40 minutes
Makes about 4 cups

1 kg green cucumbers, washed and thinly sliced
2 large white onions, cut into thin wedges
2 tablespoons salt
5 cups sugar
1 1/2 cups white wine vinegar
1 tablespoon mustard seeds
1 teaspoon turmeric
1/4 teaspoon cayenne pepper

1. Combine green cucumbers, onion wedges and salt in a bowl. Add enough water to completely cover. Let stand for 2 hours. Drain well.
2. Place sugar, vinegar, mustard seeds, turmeric

and cayenne pepper in a large heavy-based pan. Cook, stirring, over medium heat until sugar has dissolved. Add cucumber and onion mixture. Cover, reduce heat and cook gently for 10 minutes, stirring occasionally, until cucumber becomes transparent. Remove from heat.
3. Cool for 15 minutes. Spoon into sterilised jars and seal. Allow to stand for 1 week before using.

Tomato Sauce

Preparation time:
40 minutes + standing
Total cooking time:
45–55 minutes
Makes about 7 cups

2 kg ripe tomatoes, roughly chopped
4 medium brown onions, finely chopped
2 cloves garlic, roughly chopped
1 tablespoon salt
1 tablespoon black pepper
1/2 teaspoon cayenne pepper
6 whole cloves
2 cups soft brown sugar
2 cups white wine vinegar

Old-Fashioned Bread and Butter Cucumbers and Tomato Sauce.

SPICY PLUM SAUCE

Apple Apricot & Nut Chutney

1. Combine tomato, onion, garlic, salt, peppers and cloves in a large heavy-based pan. Cook gently over medium heat for 45 minutes or until soft with lots of juice.
2. Add sugar and vinegar and continue to cook over low heat until mixture thickens to sauce consistency.
3. Strain mixture through a sieve and pour into warm sterilised jars and seal. Leave Tomato Sauce for 1 week before using. Store in a cool, dry place.

Apple, Apricot and Nut Chutney

Preparation time:
  35 minutes + standing
Total cooking time:
  45 minutes
Makes about 4 cups

1 kg green apples, peeled, cored and roughly chopped
125 g dried apricots, chopped
2 medium onions, finely chopped
1 clove garlic, roughly chopped
1 cup sultanas
1/3 cup walnuts, roughly chopped
2 teaspoons salt

1/4 teaspoon cayenne pepper
1 teaspoon ground ginger
1 cup malt vinegar
1 cup soft brown sugar

1. Combine apple, apricot, onion, garlic, sultanas, walnuts, salt, pepper, ginger and vinegar in a large heavy-based pan. Cook over low heat for 5 minutes, stirring occasionally. Simmer, with lid on, for 20 minutes.
2. Add sugar, cook, stirring occasionally, for 10 minutes, uncovered, until mixture is a jam-like consistency.
3. Pour mixture into hot sterilised jars and seal immediately. Leave chutney for 2 weeks before opening.

Spicy Plum Sauce

Preparation time:
  20 minutes
Total cooking time:
  15–20 minutes
Makes about 12 cups

2 kg blood plums
1 red chilli, finely chopped
1 tablespoon salt
1 teaspoon cayenne pepper

1 teaspoon ground cloves
1 teaspoon ground allspice
1 teaspoon ground ginger
6 cups white wine vinegar
1 kg sugar

1. Cut plums in half and remove the stones.
2. Combine plums, chopped chilli, salt, cayenne pepper, cloves, allspice, ginger, vinegar and sugar in a large heavy-based pan. Bring to the boil and stir over medium heat until sugar dissolves. Continue cooking until plums are soft and mixture has slightly thickened.
3. Cool the mixture slightly and pour it, in small batches, into a food processor. Process each batch until smooth. (Test thickness of the mixture by coating the back of a spoon with it.) Pour mixture into warm sterilised jars and seal immediately.

HINT
If fresh plums are unavailable, you can use canned plums. Use plum juice from can and reduce white wine vinegar to 4 cups.

Apple, Apricot and Nut Chutney and Spicy Plum Sauce.

Index